Not Milk ... Nutmilks!

40 of the Most Original
Dairy-Free Milk Recipes Ever!

By Candia Lea Cole

Woodbridge Press

Santa Barbara, California 93160

1992

Published and distributed by

Woodbridge Press Publishing Company
Post Office Box 6189
Santa Barbara, California 93160

Printed in the United States of America

Distributed simultaneously in the United States and Canada

Library of Congress Cataloging in Publication Data:

Cole, Candia Lea.
  Not milk— nut milks! : 40 of the most original dairy-free milk recipes ever! / by Candia Lea Cole.
    p.   cm.
  Includes bibliographical references and index.
  ISBN 0-88007-184-2 : $7.95
    1. Milk-free diet—Recipes.   I. Title.
RM234.5.C65 1990
641.5′631—dc20   90-12834
                                                           CIP

Contents

List of Nutmilks

About the Author

Candia Lea Cole has been creatively involved with food preparation since she began exploring the world of vegetarianism at the age of seventeen.

Candi became keenly interested in "diet reform" when, she says, "after a personal history of ill-health that was ineffectively medicated by prescription drugs, and exacerbated by 'unconscious dietary habits,' there was nowhere else to turn to for help except back to nature."

Embarking on a whole-foods lifestyle, while learning about herbal medicine and wholistic healing principles, finally paved the way to Candi's health and heightened spiritual consciousness.

Candi has since made it her livelihood to develop innovative ways (combining aesthetic, hygienic, ethical, humane, and economic principles) of nourishing the whole body with healing gourmet foods and herbs. Her recipes emphasize the personal and planetary values of preparing foods in a manner that honors creation (the life essence) while being kind to animals and considerate of our agricultural resources.

Candi's professional interests include teaching children, teens, and adults the art and science of preparing health-enhancing cuisine, in addition to the principles of living in tune with nature. She has also managed catering services known as Gourmet Gatherings and Meals That Heal. She lives in Minnesota.

Acknowledgments

I am especially grateful for the supportive friends and acquaintances who have been present for the birth of my dietary ideas, and who have faithfully watched the fruits of my labor grow and ripen, while trusting me to find everything (and more) within myself in order to complete my books.

Those individuals include Gerald Dresow, Louise Frechette and Gary Arnold, Kate Odan O'Keefe, James Reyer, Judith Roska, Mandira Gasal, Faith O' Toole, Rick King, Bonnie Rubenstein Behr and David Behr, Dale Vanderjagt, Stanlee Willhite, Paul Juba, Anne Redpath, Dr. Paul Nash, Hal Brennan, and Mitchell Seidenfeld.

I would also like to express my appreciation to

Jean O'Hern—for seeing me "not for the woman I am, but for the angel I may be," and for her immensely giving friendship.

Marcus Thell—for meals once shared in a nutritious spirit, and for realizing when to let cocoons emerge as self-fulfilled butterflies.

Dr. Richard Barmakian—for his special impact on my health destiny and for introducing me to the beautiful blue-flowering plant, flax.

My mother Barbara—for empowering me with her courage to always be pregnant with ideas ahead of their time.

My (late) father whose "passage" has made every living moment of my life count in a whole new way.

My son Bohdan—for his sweet inspiration, and for his eager tastebuds and young helping hands, which put their stamp of approval on each and every nutmilk.

Daniel Wiemer—for his readiness and willingness to illustrate the essence of my writings in such a delicious way. Dan is a most dedicated Minneapolis artist whose talent only begins to show itself on the cover and pages of my books.

Kathy Hayes—for her nimble fingers and mind, which typed my Greek-to-her manuscripts in record time, so that they could reach their destiny.

Howard Weeks—for receiving my manuscripts in a spirit of openness, and for his warmly human approach to the business of making books for a better world.

Thomas Suttle—for his constant loving companionship, unquestioning devotion, and vigorous support of my life's work, which made it entirely possible for everything to evolve in the perfect nick of time.

From the Author

Dear Friends:

It was over a decade ago that a spark of inspiration for a "cooks" book, featuring "recipes that heal," wafted into my mind. Now, I welcome the illuminating reality of it.

This moment has surely taken a while to arrive, hasn't it? I'm inclined to believe it was waiting—waiting, that is, for myself—(and perhaps others as well) to grow in awareness of the principles for living healthfully through Nature and her wonderful world of natural foods.

Among my enjoyable moments of creating forty nutmilks, there have been *hundreds* of other meals along the way that I've chosen to envision, taste, serve, and build time to write about. Thus, a much earlier conceived book was "rebirthed" into this "easier to deliver" one, and others yet to come.

I never thought the time so long awaited to share the outcome of my labor with you would seem sweetly insignificant, but it does. What seems most meaningful today is that the interest in wholesome planetary foods shows sunny promise of being here to stay.

I'm thankful for the bits of knowledge I began to glean in yesteryears from the pioneers of the "natural foods" movement, who showed me how a little historical dietary inspiration can go a long way in inventing more of the same.

As my efforts to be inventive with new foods flourish, I'm made more profoundly aware that the food discoveries that each of us can make in our lifetimes will impact humankind for a long time to come. Prodding new awareness, they'll encourage the new kinds of nourishment our evolving bodies, minds, and spirits naturally seek.

As you taste some of the food ideas in my book(s), it is my sincere hope that you will be thoughtfully inspired to seeks ways of broadening your life-long appetites, while nourishing yourself in a creative, natural, and intimate way. Your body deserves the very best care that you alone have the ultimate potential to find and lovingly give it.

I have always considered my own exploration of whole foods the opportunity of a lifetime because it has taught me how to feel healthier, happier, and more intrinsically aware of what a balanced state of being is.

There was a time in my early dietary upbringing when I followed where the culinary path of the 1950s and 1960s led. In my teen years, I found myself complaining about a number of perplexing aches and pains symptomatic of disease. I had no real understanding of how they had culminated until I was introduced to the idea that "we are what we eat." I began to interpret the implications of such, arriving at the all-encompassing conclusion that deficiencies and imbalances in my lifestyle, including my diet of foods (and my "mental diet" of thoughts) had co-created my distressed condition.

With the help of mentors and friends much wiser than I, I was encouraged to take a new kind of responsibility for my health. It was made clear to me that the prescription drugs administered frequently during my youth were more capable of suppressing and compounding my ailments than treating them. Nature, I was informed, contained a vast pharmacy of natural healing agents—namely whole foods and herbs—that I could more safely rely on.

My mother, who had by then become as concerned as I about my past, present, and future nutritional welfare, began to seek out new-fashioned foods, a brave number of informative books on the subject of wholistic healing, and people practicing the rediscovered natural healing arts in an effort to help me recover my health.

Well, the new breed of health practitioners I was bound to visit couldn't promise me instant wellness, and the untrodden land of health food preparation didn't guarantee love at first bite. But I did find myself becoming appreciably hungry for the information being presented to me about food, nutrition, and "natural cures," as I sought clues to the cause of everything I had suffered, from jaundice and gallstones to ovarian cysts.

I knew I was being guided on a path of self-discovery and change as I developed a good habit of chewing on the ideas of several health educating authors such as Greg Brodsky, Adelle Davis, Herbert Shelton, Paavo Airola, Richard Barmakian, and many others. Each provided a meal in itself of exciting nutritional discoveries being made at the time. Eventually, I couldn't resist implementing their empirically tested health practices in my own life.

Perhaps the most valuable insight I gained after months of their revealing application, was that the human body is a miraculously functioning thing! And my own, I figured, deserved more respect than I had ever given it before.

While considering many of my lifelong dietary habits, I realized what a difficult task my body must have had for years whenever I ate haphazardly. What I mean to imply is that I didn't understand my body's nutritional needs, so I couldn't possibly nourish them accordingly.

I found that I had often naively savored foods in incompatible combinations (as many people do) and

indulged in them at times of the year when they offered
unsuitable kinds of fuel for the body's changing needs, i.e.,
noninsulating watermelon in the chill of winter, and bulk
producing oatmeal in the heat of spring and summer.

As I gradually grew more in tune with the kinds of
whole foods that Nature provides in seasonal order for the
body to sustain balance and regenerate itself (versus foods
that cause imbalance and degeneration), a more loving
appreciation of my body and Nature began to take root in
me.

I fondly recall the times during my unfolding
independent study of health when I would bring a basket
filled with a miscellany of natural foods and juices (and an
armful of books) outdoors with me to nourish my body
and thoughts. My intimate hours spent in Nature's outdoor
classroom (one very memorable spring, summer, and
autumn semester) served as a catalyst that I credit for
directing my life on a whole new course.

Mostly I attribute my breakthrough to the sun's
countenance shining upon my newly absorbent mind, the
outdoor breezes flooding my lungs with the essence of
fresh air (and cosmological energy), and a stomach content
to effortlessly digest my picnics. The unmistakable
physical energy I was gaining also promoted a mental
clarity I had never before experienced. I just couldn't help
but feel that the elements of Nature—both gross and
subtle—were empowering me to heal myself.

It wasn't long before I began to feel as if Mother
Nature herself was gently tapping on my consciousness as
if to say to me "I am here to guide you. The life essence
encompasses us. It serves us with pure energy. Just as the
intelligence of the entire universe fills each cell of the
ripened fruits and vegetables I bring you, it can be
awakened in your cells as you partake of them. Look to
me, for all that your body, mind, and spirit need, for I

function intrinsically through a Creator who has made certain that you are provided everything you could ever want to be peaceful and feel well."

Gradually the cloudy feeling that had lingered around me for many years (in which I felt separate or alone) and the feelings of powerlessness to overcome my limitations began to disperse. It became crystal clear to me that Nature was a powerfully healing friend of mine (and anyone else who cared to live interdependently with her).

The life-enhancing lesson I was learning was that "Nature lives to serve." I began to realize how we can all bring harmony to one another (and not just absent mindedly coexist) when we seek her gifts and use their healing energies to help ourselves and the planet.

Eager to bring more harmony to the earth, I fathomed the importance of my maintaining a higher level of personal energy that would sustain my physical actions while continuing to make my spirit more apparent to me.

Since my growing experience was showing me that fruits, vegetables, grains, nuts, and seeds were the easiest foods for the body to assimilate and transform into energy, I knew the energy at my command would continue to increase as I upleveled my eating experience. I also gathered that as I purified both my physical and mental bodily functions through a diet of pure foods, pure thoughts, and self-love I could reach my true health potential.

As time went on, I proved this to myself in a profound way. One day I knew—in my mind and heart—that sickness would never have to be a part of my life again as long as I lived with a cooperative spirit of personal and planetary affinity. A new found freedom and peace filled me.

In retrospect, I know that this special understanding came to me at a time when I needed it most. For my ailing body, my suffering mind, and my slumbering spirit had for many years been "wholistically aching" to know that I was more than that experience alone. My whole being was seeking its natural strength and balance and its Godgiven right to health and wholeness. Thankfully it found some of each.

Today I consider my passing health trials a rich blessing as they continue to serve a brilliant function in my infinitely healing life. I continue to seek the gifts of the earth, gathering ancient and new relics of foods and herbs together in a spirit of innovation and regeneration. The wondrous power that Nature has to create awareness and meet the body and mind's ever-changing needs is awesome.

I hope you will join me in an abundant spirit of believing we can create planetary health in our lifetime, by living in tune with the life essence.

Paraphrasing one of my favorite quotes

"What you are is God's gift to you. . . . What you are becoming is your gift to God."

May I add, God's gifts to us are the flowers, fruits, and trees. Our gift to God is what we affectionately create for ourselves and humanity with those flowers, their sweet nectar, and the fruit of the trees.

Bountiful blessings!

Candi

Once you discover the possibilities for creating a whole new foodstyle, you can discover the possibilities for creating a whole new you!

Not Milk . . . Nutmilks!

Not Milk . . .

With today's kaleidoscopic focus on healthy dietary
lifestyles, and the colorful myriad of food options that can
be explored in the process of attaining one, I have a
smiling hunch that those of you who've picked up this
book are seekers.

Chances are your dietary interests are special and you
want your food choices to match. Well, if I may say so,
"You've come to the right book!"

If you have made the choice to not drink milk, or if
you're simply becoming inclined to phase milk out of your
menus, the forty enthusiastically developed recipes herein
ought to ease you on your culinary way.

I hear more voices these days declaring healthful and
humane reasons for quenching their thirst with extra
tumblers of fresh juices, herbal teas, and dairy imposters
versus the so-called "real thing" floating in waxed cartons.
Whether or not your premises for deciding to elude such a
popular beverage first originated in your alimentary tract
or your brain, you have, according to the ongoing
newscasts reporting on modern-day milk production, made
a choice that will add years to your life.

The perilous effect of what comes from a
mechanically squeezed udder is not entirely new "news."
But it seems that it has taken a long time for an
emotionally clinging public to validate and accept this

information. If you are one of the countless individuals who has always fondly remembered milk as Nature's ideal sustenance, may I offer a simplistic commentary?

Milk, the way it once was (natural, wholesome, and unprocessed) and the way it is now (unnatural and over processed) have only one admirable characteristic in common—they are both white. However, one of those precious opaque colored liquids is virtuously capable of bringing health to the body, and the other, sicknesses. If, like me, you have resolved to keep cows milk (at least from the good old days) alive in your memory while saying grace at the dining table for the innovation of health-giving alternatives, I have a feeling we are both thinking about building a generation of more deserving nutritional ways.

Nowadays, it is more acceptable than ever before (if not a harmless touch elitist) to know precisely which eatables and drinkables do your body, mind, and emotions good. Furthermore, it is becoming downright respectable to know how the methods employed in producing the food you eat and serve can affect the well-being of our livestock, food acreage, agricultural resources, and economy.

Oftentimes I wish such issues had been more ripe for discussion during my own changing foodstyles, when the idea of sitting down to a cup of nondairy milk was practically unheard of.

It wasn't that I didn't have the pleasure of enough mealtime companions to share brunch with, but few to none of them could stop trying to convince themselves and me that "everybody" needs milk.

In my own small voice I began telling them about the "golden Guernsey" I (and an emerging handful of others) knew was not doing well, even though the dairy industry was. However, they only listened while they gulped, and I

managed to become more unsettled about the milky
moustache shading their lips. Its guise covered for my
new-found facts that it was an artificially inseminated
"solution" of hormones, chemicals, DDT, fungicides,
defoliants, and radioactive fallout (Strontium 90).[1] So
much for blue sky and green pastures.

For any among you who have not heard or read about
the modern-day preparation of milk, you may want to
"imagine" the way in which as many as 100 cows are
injected with the reproductive semen of only a few bulls.
The bulls used in this practice are often reputed to be
hurculean-sized animals that are mated with hormone-
grown "super cows" in order to produce a grossly oversized
milk sac that, more often than not, develops infections
near the cows' teats. Farmers prevent this rather
insufferable condition (which for them amounts to a
diversion of industry time and dollars) by inoculating
livestock feed with penicillin, bactracin, and other
dangerous drugs. Unfortunately the farmers' savings
threaten us as consumers since antibiotics are purported to
have an immune-suppressing function when swallowed
meal upon meal, year after year.

I realized this myself after sixteen years of drinking
milk and eating milk products, when I began to explore
some of my physical complaints with a nutritionist. The
sinusitis, allergies, respiratory weakness, and ovarian cysts
I had long suffered were linked to a deluge of scientific
research in which milk was found to lay the groundwork
for many such diseases. I was as surprised as many
individuals are when first informed that over 45 million
people in the United States alone visit diagnostic clinics
each year to receive treatment for symptoms of dairy borne

[1]These contaminants settle in the thyroid gland (particularly in children)
enabling cancers to develop. Paavo Airola, *How To Get Well*, 174.

allergies such as hay fever, eczema, asthma, and lactose intolerance (the inability to digest milk sugar). What came as an even bigger shock to me was the fact that heart disease (the *leading* cause of deaths in the United States) was linked to excessive commercial dairy product consumption—as were digestive disorders, glandular disturbances, arthritis, allergies, cavities, and more! Needless to say, I was alarmingly persuaded then, and remain healthfully convinced now, that my body (amongst others) is considerably better off without the liquid contents of cartons found in every refrigerated grocer's department in the country.

Occasionally, over the years, I have broken my rule of dietary conduct and indulged in some nicely chilled sips of raw goats milk, with the understanding that it is not milk (in and of itself) that causes the body such dietary stress; rather it is the *unnatural preparation* of it.

The famous (late) Dr. Paavo Airola, a worldwide exponent of dietary principles for healthy living, substantiates this fact in his bestselling book *How to Get Well*. In relating his lifelong diary of other foodstyle cultures in such countries as Bulgaria, Armenia, Russia, and Scandinavia, Dr. Airola noted that traditionally heavy milk drinkers were healthy and long-lived. The reasons? Such milk products were not processed by homogenization and pasteurization. According to several other health contemporaries in the United States, the most serious threat in drinking milk lies in the fact that its natural chemical structure is altered by the heat and pressure used in processing to the point of making it indigestible.

Nationally known health authority Dr. Kurt Oster contends that homogenized and pasteurized milk, which uses extreme heat and pressure to break down the normal sized fat particles (so that cream doesn't separate), causes an enzyme called *xanthine oxidase* (XO) to enter the bloodstream, which in turn destroys vital body chemicals that normally protect the arteries of the heart.[2]

Why, you may wonder, is milk still the daily choice of the general population if it poses so many serious nutritional problems? The obvious answer I see is that milk continues to be cleverly promoted by the American Dairy Association. Their advertising "magic," including singing radio broadcasts and seductive television commercials, have charmed us with the notion that "everybody needs milk," "milk does a body good," and every "baby" needs milk, so "baby yourself" a little.

After all of this, it is not exactly easy to tell a child or relative (who argues they are just trying to satisfy the requirements of the "basic four" food groups) that the liquid that makes their cereal go snap, crackle, 'n' pop at dawn and washes their cookie down at dusk is not very good for them. However, something I have proved to myself and to my own extended family circle is that it is well worth the effort to try to educate others. Enlightening conversation never hurt anyone's health and well-being. And, if you remember your place (you're not there to take anybody's milk away from them), they just may "wean" themselves.

A kiss of concern, coupled with a refreshingly chilled or cozily warmed glass of nondairy milk in their favorite flavor, may have them all in favor of the satisfying alternative—nutmilks.

Nutmilks, I have discovered, are an excellent replacement for hazardous-to-your-health dairy products, as well as being ideal, low-allergenic replacements for other nondairy milks. I couldn't be more pleased to introduce you to my "thought for food" on preparing them.

[2] "Super Health," by Dr. Kurt Donsbach Ph.D. "Hypoglycemia, Your Bondage or Your Freedom," By Dr. Richard Barmakian, N. D.

. . . Nutmilks!

Thank goodness for small kitchen appliances that make the preparation of nutmilks so easy! Nutmilks are a rare (if not unevolved) find at most supermarkets and health-food centers across the country. If you've ever gone looking for some you may have (at worst) come home empty handed or (at best) with other nondairy milks such as the increasingly popular soy- and grain-made drinks now available. Carob- and vanilla-flavored soymilks have made a big splash in the lives of vegetarians. In addition, the likes of mocha and almond-spiced grain milks (known as *Amazake* in the Orient) are inviting intrigue as well.

Of the new choices for commercially prepared nondairy milks, nutmilks have yet to make a debut in a ready-made rainbow of flavors. You can, however, scout around and find the likes of a boxed, prefabricated nut-mix preparation, consisting of roughly 99 percent chopped almonds (with guargum) which you blend with water. This very basic drink will introduce you to a nutmilk formula. But if, like me, you discover yourself calculating how its bland (and sometimes "expired") taste might be greatly improved, I know you are not going to hesitate about readying a shopping basket for more exciting ingredients.

The do-it-yourself possibilities for homemade nutmilks are endless, and by creating your own fresh and inexpensive calico collection you will be able to far exceed any great expectations of a commercially made beverage, which would probably not feature the special variety that is capable of winning tastebuds and influencing friends and family.

Since nuts and seeds, which are abundant in natural oils, tend towards rancidity, your first consideration for making truly delicious drinks will be to obtain the freshest ingredients. You will want to determine which of your local natural food co-ops or grocery markets can provide you with the finest shelled nuts. Or you may want to think of them as the edible fruit of trees and flowering plants. Once you find a reputable source, pick a generous handful of several different kinds, preferably organically grown and unsalted. If, while you are grazing, you happen to see vendors of appealing spices, flavoring extracts, natural sweeteners, or dried fruits, by all means choose a bouquet to bring home and dip your senses into.

After making a visual, oral, and tactile acquaintance with such sundries, you might find yourself imagining what a drink named Velvety Vanilla Cashew Milk tastes like. Or how about Minty Carob Pumpkin Seed Milk, Fruit Harvest Pecan Milk, or Banana Almondine?

Maybe you can envision how a handful of sweet almonds, buttery cashews, nutty pecans, or sunflower seeds is likely to be tossed into the kitchen blender at my home long before landing on a party tray atop a coffee table. You, too, may see the same thing start to happen in your household once you cordially invite your living companions to witness your culinary transformation of a nut or two.

The procedure for blending nutmilks is relatively easy. In fact, even children can learn to make them when lent a small hand of supervision. If you have a blender, an electric seed (coffee) grinder, a medium-large fine mesh strainer, and a one to two quart saucepan to heat water in, you have all the kitchen aids you need to conveniently develop recipes.

Busy but nutrition-conscious homemakers will be happy to know that the preparation time for a quart of nutmilk is only three to five minutes.* The ingredients that fall into my nutmilk blends are extra special. While only a few of the recipe suggestions I have seen for nutmilk call for "just nuts, honey, and water," the over three dozen versions herein combine several other ingredients for richer flavor, smoother texture, and greater nutritional efficacy.

A bounty of nuts and seeds form the base of my recipes and offer a concentrated food source of protein, unsaturated fats, vitamins, and minerals. I find that they are easily enhanced by natural foods offering texturous flavors, such as those in reconstituted fruit (dried apples, pears, and raisins), carob powder, nut butters, and fresh fruits. Extracts of flavor (including maple, almond, orange, vanilla, coconut, etc.) lend a special finishing touch to the milks and mingle nicely with sweeteners containing healthful properties. Maple syrup, enzyme-rich brown rice syrup, energy-giving raw honey, and the nonaddictive sweetness derived from malted grains or exotic herbaceous shrubs (such as barley malt powder and Stevia [sweet leaf] powder) are two examples that can be used in careful measure to lend a desired taste or health characteristic.

Other ingredients I use to make the difference between mediocre and marvelous sipping include high-protein flaxseed and low-cal lecithin granules. Both add synergistic fortification, as well as creamy texture via their blending of compatibly emulsifying food characteristics.

For the nutritional record, some of you may appreciate knowing that the "mighty little" northern grown flaxseed

*See time-saving suggestions on Page 57.

alone contains a desirable low-calorie, cholesterol-free supply of essential fatty acids, soluable fiber, and minerals. When moistened with water, flax is notoriously slippery and releases a healing quality that works nutritional wonders in the body.

Developing an intimacy with Nature through the foods that she offers is relatively easy, and you might find yourself doing just that as you experience the health benefits derived from your recipes.

Finally, if you are just plain zealous about health, you may want to consider stocking your kitchen pantry with uncommonly good recipe supplements such as carrot calcium powder, derived from mineral-rich carrots, and slippery elm powder, a deliciously different and healing herbal food. Along with the rest, these ingredients make unprocessed nut and seed milks richer in useable proteins, enzymes, vitamins, and minerals than any processed dairy milk on the market.

Although certain ingredients may intimidate some of you if you remain unfamiliar with their use, your ability to appreciate them can help you to make drinks that are nutritionally uncompromising, particularly if you are concerned about substituting the questionable food values of cows milk in your diet.

On the following pages, you will find all the food options available to you for the preparation of your nondairy drinks. You may want to think of the next portion of this book as a "walk-in pantry"; I call it my "nutritional sitology of ingredients." Sitology is defined as the science of food and diet. I believe we have the greatest potential to build health when we possess the knowledge.

Nutritional Sitology of Nutmilk Ingredients

High quality nutritional elements are found in abundance in nuts and seeds, which may be obtained at your local coop or health food store. Buy refrigerated nuts if you have the option.

Nutritional Sitology of Nutmilk Ingredients

Nuts and Seeds

Nuts

Nuts are the hard-shelled dry fruits or seeds of several kinds of plants, usually trees. Some readily available nuts suitable for nutmilk preparation are almonds, cashews, pecans, and walnuts. The soft inner part of the nut is called the *meat* or *kernel,* and the outer covering is called the *shell.* Nuts are a concentrated source of protein, unsaturated fat, the B complex vitamins, vitamin E, calcium, iron, potassium, magnesium, phosphorous, and copper.

Seeds

Seeds are the ripened ovules of plants. Edible seeds such as sesame, sunflower, pumpkin, and pine nuts are rich in protein. They also contain the B complex vitamins; vitamins A, D, and E; phosphorous; calcium; iron; flourine; iodine; potassium; magnesium; zinc; unsaturated fatty acids; and protein. Sesame seeds are particularly rich in calcium content, and sunflower seeds contain fifty percent protein.

The latest nutritional research shows that nuts and seeds, which are rich in essential fatty acids, can actually help the body burn unwanted fat. (See Page 47.)

Options for Sweetening Nutmilks

The following ingredients can be used alone or interchangeably to sweeten your drinks and give them the desired health value you are seeking.

Barley Malt Powder

A natural sweetener, and a fine choice for sweetening nutmilks of all flavors, barley malt powder is derived from grains that have been sprouted, dried, and cooked down to a dry natural malt. "Dr. Bronner's" (brand name) barley malt powder contains a uniquely sweet blend of barley malt, orange juice solids, calcium-magnesium-phosphate, parsley, chia seeds, vegetable protein, dulse, sea lettuce, lemon juice solids, potassium salt, rosehips, anise, and mint.

One part barley malt replaces twenty parts sugar. A dash has only three calories and substitutes for two teaspoons of sugar, giving you a reduction of up to ninety-eight percent of the usual calories without sacrificing sweetness!

Barley malt powder can be used in place of or along with liquid sweeteners. This way, you can reduce the amount of liquid sweeteners and stretch the flavor you desire.

Stevia Rebaudiana (Sweet Leaf) Powder

Stevia is an herbal sweetener, derived from a small herbaceous shrub grown in Brazil and Argentina and now in the southwestern United States. If you are on a low-sugar, low-carbohydrate, or weight-loss diet, stevia is an ingredient you will want to look into. Stevia's sweetening power is thirty to eighty times that of sugar, yet it has only one calorie per ten leaves. It can be used in the same way as barley malt powder. A pinch per cup of liquid will do.

Sweet leaf's licoricelike taste best complements nutmilks that have a minty, carob, or pumpkin flavor.

South American Indians have used this sweetener for centuries, and, although it is just becoming popular in the United States, Japanese researchers have found it to have many healthful qualities, including (1) beneficial regulating effects on blood sugar; (2) inhibitory effects on bacteria in the mouth (which aid in preventing tooth decay); (3) tonifying effects that counteract fatigue; and (4) regulating effects on metabolic functions, including diuretic properties that aid weight loss.

Stevia also contains antibacterial, antiyeast, and antifungal properties.

Honey

Because of its taste, texture, and overall availability, honey is an ingredient used in many of the nutmilk recipes herein.

Honey varies in texture, flavor, and color, depending upon the types of flowers from which the nectar is

Natural sweeteners also add nutritional value. This tasty array is available at your local coop or health food store.

gathered. As a rule, dark honeys are nutritionally superior to light honeys, although they impart a stronger flavor.

Since honey is almost twice as sweet as cane sugar, smaller amounts of it are needed for sweetening purposes.

Unfiltered raw honey contains large amounts of carbohydrates in the form of sugars, small amounts of minerals, and B complex vitamins, as well as vitamins C, D, and E.

Nutmilk recipes generally call for approximately two tablespoons of honey per quart of nutmilk. However, this amount can be adjusted to suit your needs. Less can be used with a dash of barley malt powder or stevia powder.

Maple Syrup

Good quality maple syrup (such as some authentic Canadian and Vermont versions, as well as syrup from small producers) can serve as a delicious addition to nutmilks. Although it is not particularly abundant in nutritional value, it does contain sugars, which, when used in moderation, can furnish quick energy to the body. Maple flavored extract can be used along with a lesser quantity of the syrup to impart a richer flavor. Make certain the syrup you use does not contain salt, chemical preservatives, defoaming agents, or formaldehyde (from the pellets used to tap the trees).

Brown Rice Syrup

This is a delectable liquid sweetener, pale blonde in color, resembling honey in texture and taste appeal. Rice syrup is made from organic brown rice. It is first ground into a meal, then cooked, before natural cereal enzymes are added—which convert the starches in the rice to relatively complex natural sugars. A sweet liquid is squeezed from the mixture and cooked briefly until it thickens. This is truly a nutritious sweetener, since the body does not need to release extra insulin in order to break down the *maltose* (malted grain). Its light flavor is particularly delightful in nutmilks containing fruit.

Nutmilks, already nutritious, may be super-enriched by special ingredients that are available at most food coops and health food stores.

Molasses

This is a thick syrup (light to dark brown in color) having a distinctive flavor ranging from mellow to strong.

Blackstrap molasses is the residue left after the last possible extraction of sugar from cane or beet. While it contains many nutrients, it also contains residues from the sugar growing and refining process.

Unsulphured, golden molasses (also known as West Indies Barbados molasses) is less nutritionally rich than blackstrap molasses, but it does not contain residues and is a more pleasant-tasting way to obtain iron, calcium, and traces of other vitamins and minerals.

I do not usually use molasses to flavor nutmilks, since even the golden variety imparts a strong flavor. However, it is a nutritious option.

Sucanat

Sucanat is the trade name given to a 100 percent organic granulated sugarcane juice that adds nourishment to nutmilks. Unrefined, it is considered to be a healthy alternative to refined sugar. Sucanat supplies sweet-tasting, easy-to-use calcium, phosphorus, potassium, chromium, magnesium, iron, and vitamins A and C.

Ingredients that Fortify Nutmilks

Flaxseeds

Flaxseeds are a key ingredient of nutmilks, providing fabulous food value and fiber. They are derived from the lovely blue flowering flaxseed plant that grows in the summer and is widely cultivated in the northern United States, Canada, and Europe.

Flax is a multipurpose herb, also known as *linseed*. Fiber from the stalks, along with the oil and mucilage from the seeds, have been used for centuries by weavers, painters, and beauticians as well as herbalists and cooks.

The seeds, which are chocolate brown in color, can be found at most co-ops and health food stores. The latter is likely to stock an enriched variety called Fortified Flax, made by OmegaLife, Inc. This brand assures you of an organically grown product rich in various nutritional cofactors, and minerals which aid in the effectiveness of its assimilation. Also rich in soluable fiber, flax is quite capable of replacing laxative products such as Metamucel.

Last, but not least, flaxseed contains an ingredient called *Omega* 3 which is effective in the medical treatment of various degenerative diseases in this country. Omega 3 is an essential fatty acid *(linolenic acid)* that often becomes lost in food processing. Essential to a preventative diet in the 1980s and 1990s, it is known by researchers to reduce serum tryglycerides, or "hard trans fats" as they are often called. These hard fats cannot be used as an energy source by the body as the body is unable to digest them properly.

The most noticeable effect of hard trans fats on the body is the appearance of cellulite. Hidden trans fats lodge in other areas of the body as well, such as the liver and heart, causing hardening of the liver, atherosclerosis, etc. Milk fat (from pasteurized milk) is said to contain two to eight percent trans fats that the body is ill equipped to metabolize.

Until the discovery of Omega 3's effect on the dislodging of fats from the body, it seemed there was no answer to this problem. Now, however, researchers are finding that one to three tablespoons of flax in one's daily diet can help to overcome dry skin, cellulite, constipation, colitis, ulcers, hypoglycemia, diabetes, heart disease, cholesterol, calcium deficiencies, and reproductive and immune system related disorders in a matter of a few weeks or months.[1] These nutritional discoveries certainly encouraged my culinary discoveries!

For nutmilk recipes, you'll want to experiment with one level tablespoon of ground flaxseed per quart of milk. Your task in making flax an effective ingredient in the drinks will be to first grind the seeds in an electric seed grinder until they become a fine powder. Once mixed with the other ingredients (including water), they will release a

---

[1] Unsaturated fatty acids combine with vitamin D in the body in order to make calcium available to the tissues.

mucilage that creates body and nutritional bulk. Since flaxseeds have a fibrous outer husk, you will most likely want to strain your drinks before sipping.

Lecithin

A valuable ingredient in nutmilk preparation, lecithin is a food supplement extracted from the soybean. It is an emulsifier of fats, and when combined with nuts (which are rich in fatty acids) it enhances their palatability* and aids digestion. You will find that the addition of only one teaspoon of lecithin granules per quart of nutmilk binds the ingredients, making a creamier drink.

Nutritionally speaking, lecithin plays an important part in maintaining a healthy nervous system. A natural constituent of every cell in the human body, lecithin is found in the *myelin sheath*, a fatty protective covering for the nerves. Lecithin is also known for breaking up cholesterol deposits on the arterial walls, helping to prevent heart diseases. Other reported benefits you may experience by adding lecithin to your diet include weight loss, memory improvement, and liver and kidney cleansing. Always keep lecithin granules refrigerated.

Slippery Elm Powder

Slippery elm powder is a delicious and healing herblike food used to fortify nutmilks. It is derived from the inner bark of the deciduous slippery elm tree which is grown and cultivated in North America.

Slippery elm powder has a light and fluffy texture, is pale beige in color, and may remind you of a protein powder with a maplelike aromatic quality. Although it is uncharacteristic of other dairy-, soy-, and egg-rich protein conglomerates, its food value is remarkable.

Slippery elm is as nutritious as oatmeal and possesses

*Liquid lecithin is not advisable for use in nutmilks as it alters the taste. Use the fresh granules instead.

many enzymes that aid the body's digestive processes. Its
mucilage content is soothing and healing to ailments such
as coughs, catarrh, stomach and bowel troubles, and
urinary tract irritations. It is an ideal first food for babies
or convalescing persons since it is so easy to digest. A
healthy measure of slippery elm in a banana- , maple- , or
carob-flavored nutmilk will enhance its flavor nicely as
well as add texture and nutriment.

Bee Pollen Granules

Bee pollen granules are tiny, nutritionally potent golden
food nuggets that are gathered from all kinds of flowering
plants by worker bees. The flowers' fertilizing element,
pollen, gives us the benefit of a sunpotent food rich in
natural sugars, vitamins, minerals, trace elements, amino
acids, and an estimated 5,000 enzymes! (It also contains
the complete genetic history of the plant.)

I like to add pollen (one teaspoon or less) to an
occasional blenderfull of nutmilk on days when I want a
burst of energy. Try it in a pumpkin, fruited, or carob rich
milk.

Pollen has received much recognition (health food
status) since becoming a part of the training diet of many
world class Olympic participants. It is acclaimed for its
ability to increase physical endurance and immunity, build
the blood, relieve allergies, extend life (antiaging), and
correct metabolic problems.

Calcium Carrot Powder[2]

Calcium carrot powder is a unique product available at
many health food stores. It is a white powder made from
the calcium-rich (phosphorus-free) sediment found in

---

[2]Also available: Calcium Food Malt Powder (made by "Dr. Bronner"),
which contains calcium powder and other organic sweetening ingredients.

highly mineralized soil-grown carrots. One level teaspoon supplies 950 mg of calcium. A "pinch" more is reported to supply 1,000 mg or 100 percent of the recommended daily amount of calcium, the most important mineral found deficient in many diets.

Carob Powder

Carob powder is a sweet and delicious chocolatelike powder from the fruit (pod) of an evergreen tree indigenous to the Mediterranean region. Used in nutmilks, it is a satisfying substitute for cocoa powder, which contains caffeine and other stimulants. Carob contains a fair share of protein, natural sugar, calcium, phosphorus, minerals, and B vitamins. Recent research suggests that, eaten in excess, carob may stunt childhood growth. However, these findings have not been widely substantiated. My family has eaten carob for years, and I am inclined to believe that moderation is the key, as with chocolate, cholesterol-containing foods, or anything else.

Cafix Cereal Grain Beverage Powder

Cafix is the name given to a product on the market that resembles instant coffee. Its caffeine-free, nonaddictive ingredients include mineral-rich roasted barley, rye, chicory, and shredded beet roots. Its rich flavor will "wake you" in the morning without causing sleeplessness at night. One cup of Cafix contains only seven calories. You will want to try mixing one to three teaspoons into a blender of carob-mint nutmilk for a mochalike flavor!

Special Extras

Food Flavoring Extracts

Natural nonimitation food flavorings made from the oils of natural herbs, vegetables, and fruits are available at many natural food stores. The concentrated flavoring agents contain no sugar or salt. Look for *Cook's Choice* and Frontier brands that are likely to offer a selection of orange, banana, lemon, almond, vanilla, cinnamon, coconut, butterscotch, cherry, and pineapple.*

Spices

Some of the delightful spices I use for nutmilks include cinnamon, coriander, allspice, nutmeg, mint, and anise. Spices have a long and unique history. They also have medicinal values too important to overlook. To give you an idea, cinnamon is recommended by herbalists for aiding digestion. Recent studies by Japanese researchers show that cinnamon also contains a substance that acts on certain fungi, bacteria, parasites, and botulinus. Other findings suggest other medicinal uses for cinnamon.

Anise and coriander seeds (ground) offer a pleasant-tasting way to soothe an upset stomach, aid digestion, and relieve gas.

Mint will relieve indigestion, colic, and gas and is valuable in a variety of health conditions from fevers and flu to colds, cramps, insomnia, bad breath, and abdominal pains.

Dried Fruits (Unsulfured Varieties)

A variety of dried fruits may be reconstituted for use in nutmilk recipes, and you will find that they lend nutribody to the recipes as well as unique flavors. Try apples,

*The amount of flavoring extracts in a recipe may vary, depending on the strength of the brand used.

apricots, pears, raisins, and unsulphured dates. Dried fruits contain concentrated natural fruit sugars and minerals including iron, potassium, phosphorus, and calcium.

Nut Butters and Unrefined Oils

Nut butters—such as peanut butter or almond, cashew, sunflower seed, and sesame butters—taste as rich as they sound and add a special creaminess to many nutmilks. If you forget to shop for nuts or are without a grinder to prepare them, nut butters can easily take their place.

Are Nutmilks Fattening?

No, no, no! . . . I'm happy to report. Because our bodies cannot make the essential fatty acids actually needed for fat-burning (linoleic, linolenic, and arachidonic acids), they must be obtained from our food!

With their content of flaxseed, lecithin, and oils from nuts and seeds, nutmilks are one of the best combined food sources you can give yourself. Also, fat-burning amino acids, such as arginine, tyrosine, and phenylalanine are highly concentrated in most nuts and seeds! An adequate dietary intake of these essentials can discourage deficiencies such as faulty fat metabolism, diseases of the heart or circulatory system, skin problems, and reproductive organ dysfunctions, to name a few.

Culinary Helpers

Healthful Hints and Serving Suggestions

Preparing Nutmilks in Four Easy Steps

Culinary Helpers

Here is what you will need to make nutmilk preparation a snap:

Blender—standard size, high speed model (such as Oster, Waring, Sunbeam, etc.)

Electric seed or coffee bean grinder* (such as Krups, Braun, Oster, Sunbeam, or Moulinex)

Glass, enamel, or stainless one-to-two quart stove pot.

Fine mesh strainer, 4-6″ in diameter, and stirring spoon.

Easy access refrigerator jars and pantry containers for all fresh dry nuts, seeds, spices, nut butters, sweeteners, dried fruits, and flavoring extracts.

*Consider an electric seed grinder one of the most valuable small investments you will make in a kitchen appliance. (They retail for under $20.) I wouldn't consider making nutmilks without one since it saves time in grinding nuts and seeds to the fine consistency needed for smooth, creamy drinks.

Healthful Hints and Serving Suggestions

Use Fresh, Pure Water for Your Nutmilks

Spring water, or water that has been purified by a distiller, carbon filter, or reverse osmosis unit will yield a better tasting nutmilk with a longer shelf life. In addition, its health benefits will far outweigh the risks of drinking polluted (municipal) water supplies, which test positive for heavy metals, organic chemicals and pesticides, bacteria, asbestos, and radioactive compounds—a chemical soup!

Diluted organic fruit juices can also take the place of water in some recipes. Be creative! Also, you may use cool, warm, or hot liquid for your recipes. I prefer to use warm to hot (yet not boiling) water as it emulsifies the ingredients nicely.

Use Organically Grown Ingredients

The dangers of eating commercially grown foods, with toxic sprays and additives can undo your health efforts, so you may want to explore the availability of ingredients at your local food corp.

Keep Nutmilk Ingredients Refrigerated!

Never overestimate the freshness of a nut! Especially if you buy it in a shelled, unrefrigerated state. Immediately refrigerate nuts and seeds in airtight jars when you return home from the market so as to slow the aging process of fats. Rancid nuts can actually be considered a health hazard! Taste test! An even slightly rancid nut will cause a burning sensation in the throat when eaten. You will be able to taste the difference with a little taste-bud finesse.

Get to Know Your Culinary Helpers

Spend some time experimenting with your grinder and blender. Dry nuts and oily nuts* grind up somewhat differently (you may find it works best to grind a few tablespoons at a time). Dry ground nuts will fall out of the grinder when you tip its contents into the blender. Oily ground nuts will require a cautious index finger to sweep them out. Once your milks are made, you will want to taste and see if you prefer them thinner or thicker. A day or two in the refrigerator may change their consistency slightly, and you can stir or strain them again if needed or desired.

*Dry nuts: almonds, sunflower seeds, sesame, and pumpkin seeds. Oily nuts: walnuts, pecans, cashews.

Serving Suggestions

Nut and seed milks are delicious served hot or cold. They are a nice accompaniment to breakfast cereals or snacks such as baked goods. An orange- or peanut-flavored nutmilk, for instance, has a way of doubling the pleasure of an orange muffin or a peanut butter bar or cookie. Nutmilks such as plain, almond, or vanilla cashew can be used in recipes that call for dairy milk. Shakes, smoothies, puddings, and baked goods are also enhanced by nutmilks' rich flavors and nutritive values.

Save Time

To make nutmilk preparation extra efficient, you may want to grind as much as a cup's worth of nuts/seeds (and a proportionate amount of flaxseed) at a time. Store the ground meal in airtight jars and keep refrigerated for up to a week. One cup of nuts yields three quart-size batches.

Recipes for Nut and Seed Milks

Preparing Nut and Seed Milks in Four Easy Steps

1. In a one- to two-quart saucepan, heat approximately four cups of pure water to desired temperature. Turn stove off and allow to sit while you prepare the other ingredients.
2. Select and gather refrigerated fresh nuts and flaxseed. Place approximately one fourth to one third cup of nuts in the grinder. Cover to activate grinding blades. Press and release a few times to grind the seed/nut mix, which should resemble a fine powder within about fifteen to twenty seconds. Transfer the ground mixture to a blender. Add flaxseed to grinder and repeat process. Transfer to your blender.
3. To your blender add lecithin granules, fortifiers, a sweetener of your choice, flavoring extract, and any fresh or reconstituted fruit. Then add one half to three-fourths cup of the warm or hot water (from your stove top) and blend on medium speed to a smooth, puddinglike puree. Add the remaining water suggested in the recipe and reblend on high speed until creamy.

   Use approximately three cups water per recipe for extra creamy nutmilks, and use as much as one half to three fourths cup more for a thinner version. Amounts are suggested in the recipes; you may choose to vary them, as well as the water (or juice) temperature.
4. Pour the contents of the blender through a fine mesh strainer into a bowl or pitcher. Use a spoon to stir the milk while you pour, since it will be slightly too rich to flow through the strainer without a bit of mashing.* Serve immediately or bottle and refrigerate for up to seventy-two hours.

*Food fibers strained from drinks
 may be used in baked goods recipes.

Essentially, one simple yet synergistically sound recipe can be adapted in many different ways to suit one's individual dietary needs and desires.

Almond Milks

Almonds are the browish, oval-shaped "stone" of the fruit of the almond tree, from the rose family, *Amygdalus communis*. They contain a balance of healthy proteins, fats, and carbohydrates as well as calcium, potassium, and magnesium.

Drinking nutmilks prepared with organic almond butter and almonds is one taste-pleasing way to support the health and development of teeth, bones, and muscles.

Pure and Sweet Almond Milk

1/3 c. organic raw almonds
1 Tbsp. fortified flaxseeds
1 tsp. lecithin granules
2 Tbsp. honey (or rice syrup)
1/8 tsp. almond extract
3-3 1/4 c. warm water

> *Prepare as Indicated on Page 57:*
> **Nutmilks in Four Easy Steps**

Hints

You could add fruit to this nutmilk with tasty results, or other extracts of flavor.

Thought for Food

This nutmilk is simply delicious when served chilled. The pure almond flavor is so fresh. You will easily find a few ways to serve this milk or include it in recipes that call for milk.

Apple Ginger Almond Milk

1/3 c. organic raw almonds
1 Tbsp. fortified flaxseeds
1 tsp. lecithin granules
2/3 c. red organic apple (peeled and cut)
1/4 tsp. ginger powder (adjust if desired)
1/4 tsp. coconut extract
1 Tbsp. honey
2 Tbsp. rice syrup
3 c. almost-boiling water

> *Prepare as Indicated on Page 57:*
> **Nutmilks in Four Easy Steps**

Hints

You may substitute honey with rice syrup, or vice versa. A hint more ginger powder than what is suggested will not overpower this drink. It is subtle as is.

Thought for Food

Served chilled, this nutmilk has a light and refreshing flavor. A rice cookie and a Japanese melody are all you need to complement it.

Banana Almondine Milk

1/3 c. organic raw almonds
1 Tbsp. fortified flaxseeds
1 tsp. lecithin granules
1 1/2 Tbsp. fresh almond butter
1/3 c. ripe banana
1 1/2 Tbsp. honey
1 Tbsp. sucanat
1/2–1 tsp. vanilla extract
3-3 1/4 c. almost-boiling water

> *Prepare as Indicated on Page 57:*
> **Nutmilks in Four Easy Steps**

Hints

Sucanat (a powdered pure cane sugar juice) is available at
health food stores. Almond butter develops the creamier
calcium-rich taste of this milk. East Wind's organic
almond butter is a good choice.

Thought for Food

Bananas add the nutritional benefits of potassium and iron
to this beverage and are valuable in treating various
ailments such as stomach ulcers, colitis, diarrhea,
hemmorhoids, and general lack of energy. A treat served
hot or cold.

Banana Raisin Almond Milk

1/3 c. organic raw almonds
1 Tbsp. fortified flaxseeds
1 tsp. lecithin granules
1/8–1/4 c. dark raisins (soaked)
1/3 c. ripe banana
1 Tbsp. honey
1/2 tsp. vanilla extract
3 1/4 c. warm water
dash of barley malt sweetener powder
    (optional)

> *Prepare as Indicated on Page 57:*
> **Nutmilks in Four Easy Steps**

Hints

Use a ripe banana (with brown speckled skin) for a well
developed flavor. Raisins add the benefits of an
iron-rich, strength-building food. Diluted coconut juice
could replace water.

Thought for Food

If you are weak or anemic or suffer from constipation,
catarrh, or low blood pressure, this recipe provides an easy
way to include iron-rich, strength-building foods in your
diet. Banana raisin almond milk contains super nutrition.
Consider it instant breakfast (in a glass) or serve with a
piece of raisin toast or a tart.

Mellow Carob Cocoa Almond Milk

1/4 c. organic raw almonds
1/4 c. organic raw cashew nuts
1 Tbsp. fortified flaxseeds
1 tsp. lecithin granules
2 Tbsp. carob powder
1 tsp. cocoa powder
1/2 tsp. slippery elm powder
2 1/2 Tbsp. honey (adjust if desired)
1 tsp. vanilla extract
3 1/4 c. hot water

Prepare as Indicated on Page 57:
Nutmilks in Four Easy Steps

Hints

Mixing a hint of cocoa with carob makes this taste like "authentic" hot chocolate. For variation: try ripe banana (1/2 c.) in addition to coconut extract.

Thought for Food

Served warm, this is a cozy cup of nourishment in the winter after an outing to the skating rink.

Carob Orange Elm Tree Almond Milk

1/3 c. organic raw almonds
1 Tbsp. fortified flaxseeds
1 tsp. lecithin granules
1 Tbsp. carob powder
1/2 tsp. slippery elm powder
1/4 tsp. cinnamon powder
2 1/2 Tbsp. honey
1/2 tsp. orange extract
3 1/4 c. almost-boiling water
1/8 tsp. or pinch of anise (optional)

> *Prepare as Indicated on Page 57:*
> **Nutmilks in Four Easy Steps**

Hints

I use Cook's Choice brand orange extract. The slippery elm powder always adds a nice healing quality to the drinks.

Thought for Food

This milk brings a conversational cup of flavor to time shared with someone special.

Mocha Mint Almond Milk

1/3 c. organic raw almonds
1 Tbsp. fortified flaxseeds
1 tsp. lecithin granules
2 Tbsp. carob powder
2 tsp. Cafix cereal grain beverage
    powder
2 1/2 Tbsp. honey
1/4 tsp. mint extract
3 1/4 c. almost-boiling water
dash of barley malt sweetener powder
    (optional)

> *Prepare as Indicated on Page 57:*
> **Nutmilks in Four Easy Steps**

Hints

Stevia sweet leaf powder could replace a portion of the sweetener in this milk, if desired.

Thought for Food

If you like the gourmet appeal of coffee and chocolate, this mineral-rich drink will offer you a delicious caffeine-free replacement.

Orange Fresh Almond Milk

1/3 c. organic raw almonds
1 Tbsp. fortified flaxseeds
1 tsp. lecithin granules
1/2 tsp. slippery elm powder
3 Tbsp. pure maple syrup
1/2 tsp. orange extract
3-3 1/4 c. almost-boiling water

> *Prepare as Indicated on Page 57:*
> **Nutmilks in Four Easy Steps**

Hints

I use Cook's Choice brand orange extract.

Variation: Substitute maple with honey and replace elm powder with Cafix cereal beverage powder.

Thought for Food

Whichever way you serve this milk it is sure to be a taste pleaser!

Raspberry Almond-Butter Milk

1/3 c. organic raw almonds
1 Tbsp. fortified flaxseeds
1 tsp. lecithin granules
1 1/2 Tbsp. almond butter (roasted)
3 Tbsp. raspberry jelly
1 1/2 Tbsp. honey
1/2 tsp. vanilla extract
3-3 1/4 c. almost-boiling water

> *Prepare as Indicated on Page 57:*
> **Nutmilks in Four Easy Steps**

Hints

The most delicious organic almond butter I've sampled is one called Amandes de Jardin, imported from Jardine Organic Ranch in Paso Robles, California. You may want to use seedless raspberry jelly. Sorrel Ridge brand was used in this drink.

Thought for Food

Almonds are notoriously rich in calcium, and this nutmilk offers a smooth way to assimilate it.

Almond butter (with jelly) is a favorite with kids and can substitute for peanut butter if one is allergic to it.

Cashew Milks

Golden cashew nuts are actually the embryo-shaped fruit of the tropical American Tree (*Anacardium occidentale* from the cashew family Anacardicae)

The savory cashew nut and nut butter are great body builders and easily digested when eaten raw. Organic cashew nuts make a nicely textured nutmilk and are a healthy source of calories, phosphorus, and calcium. If you want to increase your vitality or find nutritional ways to prevent teeth and gum problems, cashew milk will reward your efforts.

Golden Apricot Cashew Milk

1/3 c. organic raw cashew nuts
1 Tbsp. fortified flaxseeds
1 tsp. lecithin granules
1/4–1/3 c. dried (unsulphured) apricots
    (rehydrated)
2 1/2 Tbsp. honey
1 tsp. vanilla extract
1/4 tsp. orange extract
3 1/4-3 1/2 c. almost-boiling water
dash of barley malt sweetener powder or
pinch of sucanat (optional)

> *Prepare as Indicated on Page 57:*
> **Nutmilks in Four Easy Steps**

Hints

Soak apricots overnight in dish of pure water, or pour almost boiling water over them and let stand for thirty minutes before blending.

Thought for Food

Apricots add the benefit of vitamin A, iron, calcium, and potassium, which makes them beneficial in cases of anemia, tuberculosis, and asthma. The golden fruit can also help with weight loss, toxemia, and blood impurities.

    The nourishing combination in this drink makes it a good before- or after-workout drink.

Blueberry Cashew Milk

1/3 c. organic raw cashews
1/8 c. almonds
1 Tbsp. fortified flaxseeds
1 tsp. lecithin granules
1/3–2/3 c. blueberries
2 1/2 Tbsp. honey
1 tsp. vanilla extract
3 + c. almost-boiling water
1/2 c. coconut milk (optional)

> *Prepare as Indicated on Page 57:*
> **Nutmilks in Four Easy Steps**

Hints

I blend sweet almonds and smooth textured cashews for nutrition and flavor; a touch of coconut milk adds a mellow fruitiness to the blueberries. Summer Song or Lakewood brand coconut milk contain pear and grape flavors.

Thought for Food

Blueberries are a natural blood cleanser. They have an antiseptic value that is capable of soothing inflammation in the intestines. They are also recommended for cases of anemia, constipation, overweight conditions, and complexion problems. If you like blueberries, this drink should be especially pleasing.

Carob Butter Cashew Milk

1/3 c. organic raw cashew nuts
1 Tbsp. fortified flaxseeds
1 tsp. lecithin granules
1 Tbsp. carob powder
3/4 Tbsp. creamy peanut butter
2 Tbsp. honey
1 tsp. vanilla extract
3 1/4 c. almost-boiling water
dash of barley malt sweetener powder
    (optional)

> *Prepare as Indicated on Page 57:*
> **Nutmilks in Four Easy Steps**

Hints

I use unsalted, nonhydrogenated, no-additive peanut
butter when available. It is easier to digest.

Thought for Food

Peanut butter is made from a bean (*legume*) although it is
often referred to as a nut butter. Its high-protein, high-fat
content make it desirable if you are underweight or have
low blood pressure.

    This milk is usually a hit with children since it
contains the flavors their bodies so often crave.

Lemon Coconut Cashew Milk

1/3 c. organic raw cashew nuts
1 Tbsp. fortified flaxseeds
1 tsp. lecithin granules
2 Tbsp. fresh, raw unsweetened
    shredded coconut or 1/8 tsp
    coconut extract
3 Tbsp. golden brown rice syrup
1 tsp. Hain brand "All Blend" oil
1/2 tsp. lemon extract
3-3 1/4 c. almost-boiling water
dash of barley malt sweetener powder
    (optional)

Prepare as Indicated on Page 57:
Nutmilks in Four Easy Steps

Hints

Coconut should be ground to as fine a meal as possible using an electric seed grinder for a smooth (not grainy) milk.

A fine lemon extract, is Cook's Choice brand. Rice syrup (rather than honey) really makes a sweet difference in this recipe. Westbrae or Yinnies brand syrups are available at co-ops and health stores.

Thought for Food

Coconut adds the benefit of organic iodine and protein, which can help prevent thyroid problems and ease constipation and gas in the intestines.

Lemon coconut milk might just remind you of dessert in a glass!

Mock Eggnog Cashew Milk

1/3 c. organic raw cashew nuts
1 Tbsp. fortified flaxseeds
1 tsp. lecithin granules
3/4–1 tsp. grated lemon rind
Scant 1/2 tsp. nutmeg powder
2–3 Tbsp. honey
1 1/2 tsp. vanilla extract
3-3 1/4 c. almost-boiling water
dash of cinnamon
dash of barley malt sweetener powder or
     pinch of sucanat (optional)

> *Prepare as Indicated on Page 57:*
> **Nutmilks in Four Easy Steps**

Hints

I use unsprayed organic lemon rind.

Choose your vanilla extract with care to bring the best out of this nutmilk.

Thought for Food

Mock eggnog milk is a delicious way to make any day seem like a holiday. I like it best chilled.

Maple Sunshine Cashew Milk

1/3 c. organic raw cashew nuts
1 Tbsp. fortified flaxseeds
1 tsp. lecithin granules
1/2 tsp. slippery elm powder
2–3 Tbsp. pure maple syrup
1/4–1/2 tsp. orange extract
3-3 1/4 c. almost-boiling water

> *Prepare as Indicated on Page 57:*
> **Nutmilks in Four Easy Steps**

Hints

Just a hint of orange extract is enough to let the flavor of "sunshine" through each sip.

Thought for Food

Served hot or cold, this luscious nutmilk offers a creamy, rich accompaniment to breakfasts and snacks. How about an orange-blossom muffin or an anise-flavored cookie with it?

Mellow Maple Cashew Milk

1/3 c. organic raw cashew nuts
1 Tbsp. fortified flaxseeds
1 tsp. lecithin granules
2 Tbsp. fresh creamy cashew butter
2 Tbsp. honey
1/2 tsp. maple extract
3 1/4 c. almost-boiling water
dash of barley malt sweetener powder or
      pinch of sucanat (optional)

> *Prepare as Indicated on Page 57:*
> **Nutmilks in Four Easy Steps**

Hints

Cashew butter is available at natural food stores and well worth the shopping trip.

    A fine maple extract is Cook's Choice brand.

Thought for Food

Maple cashew milk is a treat anytime, whether a la carte or in recipes (perhaps a pudding, frosting, or batter). You might even enjoy it as a nightcap.

Soft Peach Cashew Milk

1/3 c. organic raw cashew nuts
1 Tbsp. fortified flaxseeds
1 tsp. lecithin granules
2 medium small fresh peeled peaches
2–3 Tbsp. honey
1/2 tsp. vanilla extract
1/8–1/4 tsp. orange extract
3 1/4 c. almost-boiling water
dash of barley malt sweetener powder
        (optional)

> *Prepare as Indicated on Page 57:*
> **Nutmilks in Four Easy Steps**

Hints

I use ripe organic peaches to obtain the best flavor. A fine brand of vanilla and orange extract is Cooks Choice.

Thought for Food

Peaches add the benefits of vitamins, minerals, and health values useful in the treatment of anemia, a dull or spoiled complexion, constipation, high blood pressure, bronchitis, asthma, and toxicity of the body in general.

Soft peach milk is delightful when chilled, or serve warm for a cool-weather breakfast drink.

Prairie Flower and Fruit Cashew Milk

1/3 c. organic raw cashew nuts
1 Tbsp. fortified flaxseeds
1 tsp. lecithin granules
1 medium red apple, peeled and sliced
2 Tbsp. honey
1/4–1/2 tsp. lemon extract
3 c. almost-boiling water

> *Prepare as Indicated on Page 57:*
> **Nutmilks in Four Easy Steps**

Hints

A sweetish, organic apple is nice in this drink and attracts the flavor of refreshing lemon. Cook's Choice brand lemon extract is available at co-ops and health food stores.

Thought for Food

An apple adds the benefits of vitamins, minerals, and cleansing values, which strengthen the blood and clear away such conditions as constipation, catarrh, halitosis, obesity, gallstones, intestinal toxins (poor digestion), and complexion problems.

This milk has a fresh light taste and might be just the thing to take the place of coffee or juice with your fruit croissant.

Velvety Vanilla Cashew Milk

1/3 c. organic raw cashew nuts
1 Tbsp. fortified flaxseeds
1 tsp. lecithin granules
2 Tbsp. honey
1 1/2–2 tsp. vanilla extract
3-3 1/4 c. warm water
pinch of cinnamon or cardamom
        powder (optional)

Prepare as Indicated on Page 57:
Nutmilks in Four Easy Steps

Hints

Whole, raw, organic cashews will insure the simple
elegance of this basic recipe as will a good quality vanilla.

Thought for Food

This vanilla milk is a delight on its own, or as a nondairy
base for recipes such as fruit smoothies, puddings, or
baked goods. It is also a fine topping for cereals (chilled)
and may be the simplest milk to make when you need a
quick beverage to go with a bar or cookie.

Pecan Milks

A botanical name associated with the tree-grown, butterscotch-colored pecan nut is *Hicoria*.

Fresh raw pecans have a luxuriously rich taste and are suppliers of calcium, phosphorus, potassium, and essential oils.

The pecan is valuable for the dietary treatment of low blood sugar and general weakness. It can also contribute to a healthy smile. Blended into nutmilks, pecans cannot help but contribute to your health.

Apple Fruit Harvest Pecan Milk

1/3 c. organic raw pecans
1 Tbsp. fortified flaxseeds
1 tsp. lecithin granules
2/3 c. dried (unsulphured) apples
    (rehydrated)
1/2 tsp. cinnamon powder
1/4 tsp. anise powder
2–3 Tbsp. golden brown rice syrup
3-1/2 c. hot water or very diluted apple juice
1 tsp.–1 Tbsp. of sucanat (optional)

> *Prepare as Indicated on Page 57:*
> **Nutmilks in Four Easy Steps**

Hints

Sucanat—an unprocessed, powdered, pure cane sugar juice—is available at health food stores. The natural sweetness, vitamins, and minerals are condensed in dried apples and just a bit of soaking activates nutrients and flavor galore!

Thought for Food

I love this nutmilk, with its mellow rich nectary of dessertlike flavors. Rice syrup, cinnamon, and apples were made for each other! An apple tart, muffin, or croissant complement this milk.

Banana Cream Pecan Milk

1/3 c. organic raw pecans
1 Tbsp. fortified flaxseeds
1 tsp. lecithin granules
1/2 tsp. slippery elm powder
1/2–2/3 c. homemade dehydrated
    bananas (rehydrated)
2 Tbsp. maple or brown rice syrup
3-1/2 c. almost-boiling water
dash of spices, such as cinnamon and
    nutmeg

> *Prepare as Indicated on Page 57:*
> **Nutmilks in Four Easy Steps**

Hints

An electric food dehydrator with cross airflow dries bananas beautifully and is the secret to this creamy tasting milk.

To Prepare: Peel ripe bananas. Find small dip in the end of the fruit, gently press finger into end and split banana in three long banana shaped segments. They are dry when leathery yet pliable.

Thought for Food

The protein and carbohydrates in this milk are capable of sustaining your energy for hours!

Caramel Date Pecan Milk

1/3 c. organic raw pecans
1 Tbsp. fortified flaxseeds
1 tsp. lecithin granules
1/3 c. barhi dates (pitted)
1 tsp. cashew butter and/or 1 tsp. soft
    butter
1 Tbsp. sucanat
1/8 tsp. butterscotch extract (adjust;
    optional)
1/2 tsp. vanilla extract
3 1/4 c. hot water

Prepare as Indicated on Page 57:
Nutmilks in Four Easy Steps

Hints

Barhi dates are usually quite soft and do not require presoaking. They have a delicious caramel-like flavor

Thought for Food

This milk is so simple to make, yet so unique in its appeal. Great with a butterscotch brownie!

Crescent Fruit Pecan Milk

1/3 c. organic raw pecans
1 Tbsp. fortified flaxseeds
1 tsp. lecithin granules
1/2 tsp. slippery elm powder
1/8 c. soaked dates
1/3 c. ripe banana
2 Tbsp. honey or sucanat
3 1/4 c. warm water
1/2 tsp. vanilla extract

> *Prepare as Indicated on Page 57:*
> **Nutmilks in Four Easy Steps**

Hints

I use soft, pitted organic dates in this drink. Soak dates in a bit of near-boiling water for fifteen minutes if you forgot to rehydrate them overnight. Very diluted pear juice could replace water.

Thought for Food

Bananas provide the body with iron and potassium. In addition, their healing fibers can soothe ulcers, colitis, and intestinal inflammation in general.

Sending the people you love to work or play, with this drink in their bodies, will leave a good feeling in yours as well.

Maple Pecan Milk

1/3 c. organic raw pecans
1 Tbsp. fortified flaxseeds
1 tsp. lecithin granules
1/2 tsp. slippery elm powder
3 Tbsp. pure maple syrup
1/2 tsp. vanilla extract
3 1/4 c. almost-boiling water
1/4 tsp. cinnamon (optional)
pinch of sucanat (optional)

> *Prepare as Indicated on Page 57:*
> **Nutmilks in Four Easy Steps**

Hints

With its aromatic quality, highly nourishing slippery elm powder blends nicely with maple syrup. If desired, you can use less syrup, replacing it with a dash of barley malt sweetener powder and maple extract.

Thought for Food

This milk might just be the thing to serve with a pancake breakfast.

Pine Nut Milks

Pine nuts or "pinion nuts" as they are sometimes called, are the rather petite and pretty cream-colored seeds of any of several pine trees.

Digesting pine nuts raw, as in a nutmilk, provides the body with vitamins A and B in addition to calcium and iron.

Pine nuts are also rich in essential oils and healthy calories which make them desirable if you are an active person or need to build strength and energy.

Sunkissed Fruit and Pine Nut Milk

1/3–1/2 c. organic raw pine nuts
1 Tbsp. fortified flaxseeds
1 tsp. lecithin granules
1/8–1/4 c. golden yellow raisins (soaked)
2–2 1/2 Tbsp. rice syrup or honey
1/8 tsp. orange extract
3-3 1/4 c. warm water

> *Prepare as Indicated on Page 57:*
> **Nutmilks in Four Easy Steps**

Hints

Golden raisins add a slightly fruitier taste to this milk, especially with the addition of orange extract. Diluted apple cider could replace water.

Thought for Food

There is nothing like this nutritious kiss of flavor that you may never have tasted before.

Ginger Sweet Pine Nut Milk

1/3 c. organic raw pine nuts
1 Tbsp. fortified flaxseeds
1 tsp. lecithin granules
1/4–1/2 tsp. ginger powder (adjust to taste)
1/8 tsp. cinnamon
1/8 tsp. allspice
1 1/2 Tbsp. light molasses
1 Tbsp. honey
1 Tbsp. sucanat
1/4 tsp. lemon extract
3-3 1/4 c. almost-boiling water
1 tsp. butter (optional)

Prepare as Indicated on Page 57:
Nutmilks in Four Easy Steps

Hints

Lemon extract and ginger powder blend nicely in this
rather unique tasting milk. You can serve it hot or chilled.
I prefer it warmed.

Thought for Food

I prepared this milk one evening when I wanted to satisfy a
dessert-craving for gingerbread.

Peanut Butter and Strawberry Pine Nut Milk

1/3 c. organic raw pine nuts
1 Tbsp. fortified flaxseeds
1 tsp. lecithin granules
1 1/2 Tbsp. organic peanut butter
2 1/2–3 Tbsp. organic strawberry
     conserves
1 Tbsp. honey (adjust as desired)
1/2–1 tsp. vanilla extract
3 1/4 c. almost-boiling water

> *Prepare as Indicated on Page 57:*
> **Nutmilks in Four Easy Steps**

Hints

Smooth style peanut butter works best for blending this milk. I use Cascadia Farm brand jelly available at food co-ops and health food stores.

Thought for Food

Kids will guess the flavors in this after a couple of tasty sips. I sure like the idea of preparing food with organic ingredients!

Sweet Pear and Pine Nut Milk

1/3 c. organic raw pine nuts
1 Tbsp. fortified flaxseeds
1 tsp. lecithin granules
1/3 c. dried (unsulphured) pears
   (rehydrated)
2 tsp. carob powder
2 1/2 Tbsp. honey
1/8–1/4 tsp. mint extract
3 1/2 c. almost-boiling water
dash of cinnamon

> *Prepare as Indicated on Page 57:*
> **Nutmilks in Four Easy Steps**

Hints

Soak pears in almost boiling water for 1/2 hour before blending, or soak overnight. You could substitute part of the honey with barley malt sweetener powder.

Thought for Food

Mineral-rich dried pears and carob powder make this a nutritious choice!

Creamy Pineapple Pine Nut Milk

1/3 c. organic raw pine nuts
1 Tbsp. fortified flaxseeds
1 tsp. lecithin granules
1/2 c. crushed pineapple
1/4 c. ripe banana, mashed
2 Tbsp. organic brown rice syrup
1 Tbsp. honey
1/4–1/2 tsp. orange extract
1/4 tsp. vanilla extract
3 1/4-3 1/3 c. almost boiling water

Prepare as Indicated on Page 57:
Nutmilks in Four Easy Steps

Hints

I used canned pineapple (crushed in its own juice), for this milk, but if you have a sweet, fresh pineapple, you could use it instead.

Remember to be absolutely certain your pine nuts are fresh (refrigerated always).

Thought for Food

This milk, with its potassium, magnesium and mineral-rich banana content and its enzyme-rich pineapple juice, is nutritious and easy to digest. Serve it chilled to flatter the taste of each ingredient. With drinks like this . . . who needs piña coladas?

Walnut Milks

Walnuts are the nuts from trees of the genus *Juglans*.
Abundant in vitamins, minerals, and essential oils,
walnuts are helpful in alleviating constipation and liver
ailments, and they strengthen the muscles. Combined
with other nutritious delicious ingredients, the benefits of
walnuts are simply multiplied.

Banana Coconut Cream Walnut Milk

1/3 c. organic raw walnuts
1 Tbsp. fortified flaxseeds
1 tsp. lecithin granules
2/3 c. ripe banana (mashed)
2 Tbsp. honey
1 Tbsp. rice syrup
1/2 tsp. coconut extract
1/2 tsp. vanilla extract
3 1/4 c. almost-boiling water

Prepare as Indicated on Page 57:
Nutmilks in Four Easy Steps

Hints

You could use either all honey for sweetening or all rice syrup, depending upon your preference.

Thought for Food

I served this pleasant nutmilk flavor combination to a rather finicky child whose palate was developed on cows milk, and he has never stopped asking me to "make it again."

Blackberry Banana Walnut Milk

1/3 c. organic raw walnuts
1 Tbsp. fortified flaxseeds
1 tsp. lecithin granules
1/8 c. blackberries
2/3 c. ripe banana (mashed)
1 tsp. almond butter
1/8 tsp. cinnamon
2 1/2–3 Tbsp. honey
3 1/4–3 1/2 c. almost-boiling water

> *Prepare as Indicated on Page 57:*
> **Nutmilks in Four Easy Steps**

Hints

I use frozen blackberries in this milk. You will find they add a bit of tangy flavor and purplish color.

A dash of carob or slippery elm could also be added.

Thought for Food

This milk is uncharacteristic of my other nutmilks, but tasty just the same, especially if chilled. Drink it all by itself for quick nourishment, or try using it as a nondairy base blended with a frozen banana to make a "smoothie"!

Coconut Date and Walnut Milk

1/3 c. organic raw walnuts
1 Tbsp. fortified flaxseeds
1 tsp. lecithin granules
1/3–2/3 c. soaked chopped dates
1 Tbsp. rice syrup or honey (adjust as
    desired)
1 1/2 tsp. vanilla extract
1/4 tsp. orange extract or 1/4 tsp.
    coconut extract
3 1/3 c. almost-boiling water
2 Tbsp. raw unsweetened shredded
    coconut (optional)

Prepare as Indicated on Page 57:
Nutmilks in Four Easy Steps

Hints

If you choose, you can use coconut extract instead of
ground coconut flakes (which sometimes add graininess to
the drink unless its ultrastrained.) You may wish to
experiment with the flavor variations a bit.

Thought for Food

Dates are a concentrated, yet nourishing carbohydrate
food and are easily digested. They have been found
valuable in the nutritional treatment of anemia, low blood
pressure, ulcers, colitis, tuberculosis, and nervous and
respiratory conditions. Drink to your health!

Fruit Jewel and Carob Walnut Milk

1/3 c. organic raw walnuts
1 Tbsp. fortified flaxseeds
1 tsp. lecithin granules
1 Tbsp. creamy sesame tahini nut butter
1/4 c. soaked medjhool dates or raisins
1 small red apple (peeled and sliced)
2 Tbsp. carob
2 1/2 Tbsp. honey (adjust as desired)
3 1/3 c. almost-boiling water
1/2 tsp. vanilla (optional)

> *Prepare as Indicated on Page 57:*
> **Nutmilks in Four Easy Steps**

Hints

Use a sweet (rather than tart) apple for this drink.
   Variation: Omit apple and/or dates and add 1/3 to
1/2 c. ripe banana with vanilla flavoring to taste.

Thought for Food

Every ingredient in this drink carries nutritional weight.

Pumpkinseed Milks

Crunchy, earthen-green pumpkin seeds come to us in bountiful supply from the mothering pumpkin vine known as *Cucurbita Pepo*. Pumpkin seeds contain nutrients such as phosphorus, iron, calcium, and vitamin A, as well as nutritional factors that nourish the prostate gland and aid in male hormone production. Females should not pass these seeds by, however, since they are also reliable body builders and intestinal regulators.

Minty Carob Pumpkinseed Milk

1/3 c. organic pumpkinseeds
1 Tbsp. fortified flaxseeds
1 tsp. lecithin granules
2 Tbsp. carob powder
2 Tbsp. honey
2 tsp. unrefined oil (such as Hain's All
    Blend); (optional)
1/4 tsp. mint extract
3–3 1/4 c. hot water
dash of barley malt sweetener powder
    (optional)

> *Prepare as Indicated on Page 57:*
> **Nutmilks in Four Easy Steps**

Hints

This recipe will succeed without the oil, although it seems to add a creamier quality to the drink.

Stevia sweet leaf powder can also be used to sweeten this drink.

Thought for Food

Minty carob pumpkinseed milk has a refreshing taste, chilled or hot. A scoop of ice cream in the hot version creates an instant dessert drink you may want to share with a friend.

Chocolate Mountain Pumpkinseed Milk

1/3 c. organic raw pumpkinseeds
1 Tbsp. fortified flaxseeds
1 tsp. lecithin granules
2 1/2–3 Tbsp. fruit-sweetened chocolate
  sauce
1 Tbsp. honey
1 tsp. vanilla extract
1/8 tsp. mint extract
3 1/4 c. almost-boiling water

> *Prepare as Indicated on Page 57:*
> **Nutmilks in Four Easy Steps**

Hints

A delightfully healthful brand of chocolate sauce
containing pineapple juice, unsweetened Dutch cocoa,
concentrated pear and peach juices, and pure vanilla is
Chocolate Mountain Brand, distributed by Barbara's
Bakery from California.

Thought for Food

This nutmilk is rich and yummy and less apt to produce
the guilt that an artificially embalmed chocolate dairy milk
might.

Sweet Fruit-of-the-Vine Pumpkinseed Milk

1/3 c. organic raw pumpkinseeds
1 Tbsp. fortified flaxseeds
1 tsp. lecithin granules
1/3 c. pureed pumpkin
2–3 Tbsp. honey (vary with sweetener below*)
1 tsp. cinnamon
1/4 tsp. anise (adjust as desired)
1 1/2 tsp. vanilla extract
3 1/3 c. warm water
*dash of Dr. Bronners barley malt
    sweetener powder or pinch of
    sucanat (optional)

> *Prepare as Indicated on Page 57:*
> **Nutmilks in Four Easy Steps**

Hints

I use canned pumpkin in this recipe unless I have autumn leftovers on hand. Sucanat is extra tasty in this beverage.

Thought for Food

Pumpkin contains lots of vitamin A and potassium as well as healthy carbohydrates. The yellow fruit is capable of nourishing the spleen and will soothe inflamed intestines, stomach ulcers, and hemorrhoids. According to nutritionists, it can also raise low blood pressure and carry nourishment to the body.

If you like spices, you will like this nutmilk. Enjoy with a pumpkin cookie or bar, or consider it a high-protein breakfast drink (chilled). Served warm, it makes one appreciate seasonable garden tidings.

Rice Nectar Pumpkinseed Milk

1/3 c. organic raw pumpkinseeds
1 Tbsp. fortified flaxseeds
1 tsp. lecithin granules
1/2 c. ripe banana (mashed)
1/4 tsp. cardamom
3 Tbsp. organic brown rice syrup
1 tsp. vanilla extract
3-3 1/4 c. warm water

> *Prepare as Indicated on Page 57:*
> **Nutmilks in Four Easy Steps**

Hints

I used golden-blonde-colored rice syrup in this milk (made by Lundberg Farms). It has a mellow sweetness (not as concentrated as honey) and nicely enhances the banana's sweet nourishment.

Thought for Food

The little bit of spice in this nutmilk lends it a rich touch of flavor. Serve it warmed (as a nightcap) or chilled anytime you crave something good for you!

Sesame Seed Milks

Sesame seeds are derived from an East Indian herb also known as *gama grass*.

Sesame seeds and sesame butter are richly abundant in calcium and contain a share of potassium, phosphorus, and vitamin E.

The vitamin E content in the seeds is said to strengthen the heart, liver, and nerves. If you suffer with constipation, an underweight condition, or have undesireable local swellings or tumors, sesame seeds can offer nutritional help. They are also extremely beneficial for lactating women when the body's demand for calcium is particularly high.

Clover Honey and Sesame Seed Milk

1/3 c. organic raw cashew nuts
1 Tbsp. fortified flaxseeds
1 1/2 Tbsp. sesame tahini nut butter
3 Tbsp. honey
2 1/2 tsp. vanilla extract
3-3 1/4 c. almost-boiling water

Prepare as Indicated on Page 57:
Nutmilks in Four Easy Steps

Hints

I use a light rather than dark honey for a greater emphasis on the sesame.

Thought for Food

The simple flavors come through in this milk, as does its nourishing calcium content.

This drink and a sesame halvah bar go hand in hand!

Creamy Sesame and Sunflower Seed Milk

1/3 c. organic raw sunflower seeds
1 Tbsp. fortified flaxseeds
1 tsp. lecithin granules
2–3 tsp. sesame tahini nut butter
1/3 c. ripe banana (mashed)
2–2 1/2 Tbsp. honey or rice syrup
1 tsp. vanilla extract
3 1/4–3 1/3 c. warm water

> *Prepare as Indicated on Page 57:*
> **Nutmilks in Four Easy Steps**

Hints

I use Arrowhead Mills brand organic sesame tahini in this milk. Diluted cider or pear juice can replace water.

Thought for Food

Sunflower and sesame are the "King" and "Queen" of nourishing seeds. You will be able to taste and feel their virtues.

Raisin Valencia Nut and Sesame Seed Milk

1/3 c. organic raw sunflower seeds
1 Tbsp. fortified flaxseeds
1 tsp. lecithin granules
1 tsp. sesame tahini nut butter
1 tsp. smooth organic peanut butter
1 1/2 Tbsp. honey (adjust as desired)
2 Tbsp. raisins (soaked)
1/8 c. (small chunk) of ripe banana
1 1/2 tsp. vanilla extract
3 1/4 c. almost-boiling water
dash of barley malt sweetener powder
    (optional)

Prepare as Indicated on Page 57:
Nutmilks in Four Easy Steps

Hints

You can add more raisins to this recipe if desired. A pinch of coriander (ground spice) is also an option.

Thought for Food

You can use this milk in a recipe for baked goods, or kids might like it served cold with peanut butter sandwiches.

Sunflower Seed Milks

Sunflower seeds—those small, greyish edible gems that peek out from the flowering heads of the tall, proud summertime plant of the genus *Helianthus*—are a wonderfully balanced whole food.

Raw, organically grown seeds ought to be a part of everyone's diet (especially vegetarians) since they nourish the entire body. Their near-complete protein content, plus vitamins and minerals, provide the body with many nutrients needed for growth and repair. If you suffer with weak eyes, poor fingernails, tooth decay, lackluster skin and hair, or arthritis, sunflower seed milk on your menus can pleasantly help to change these conditions within a very short time.

Cinnamon Spiced Sunflower Seed Milk

1/3 c. organic raw sunflower seeds (see
mint)
1 Tbsp. fortified flaxseeds
1 tsp. lecithin granules
2 Tbsp. honey
1/4 tsp. cinnamon
1 tsp. vanilla extract
3–3 1/4 c. almost-boiling water
dash of barley malt sweetener powder or
pinch of sucanat (optional)

> *Prepare as Indicated on Page 57:*
> **Nutmilks in Four Easy Steps**

Hints

For a roasted version of this drink, try using fresh,
unsalted, toasted sunflower seeds and add 2 teaspoons
carob powder.

Thought for Food

This sunflower seed milk has a distinctive "earthy" taste
and sweet nutritive value.

Sunflower seed nutmilks are best when served within
twenty-four to forty-eight hours.

Golden Minerals Sunflower Seed Milk

1/3 c. organic raw sunflower seeds
1 Tbsp. fortified flaxseeds
1 tsp. lecithin granules
1 Tbsp. light Barbados molasses
1 tsp. carob powder
1/3 c. ripe banana (mashed)
2 Tbsp. honey
1/2–1 tsp. vanilla extract
3–3 1/4 c. almost-boiling water

Prepare as Indicated on Page 57:
Nutmilks in Four Easy Steps

Hints

Be sure to use light rather than dark molasses.

Thought for Food

This sunflower milk has plenty of the calcium and iron
everybody needs. You could cool down a creamy bowl of
hot cereal with it.

High Protein Sunflower Seed Sprout Milk

1/3 c. 12 + hour sunflower seed sprouts
1/3 c. organic raw sunflower seeds
1 Tbsp. fortified flaxseeds
1 tsp. lecithin granules
2 1/2 Tbsp. honey
1 1/2 tsp. vanilla extract
3 1/4–3 1/3 c. almost-boiling water

> *Prepare as Indicated on Page 57:*
> **Nutmilks in Four Easy Steps**

Hints

Sprouting sunflower seeds increases their vitamin and enzyme content a hundred fold!

To Sprout: Thoroughly rinse and drain 1 c. sunflower seeds. Put into a small (16 oz.) earthen bowl or Tupperware container. Cover seeds with pure water; add two inches more water. Let seeds absorb water for twelve hours or more. Seeds will become crunchier (more "raw") and begin to bud a *tiny* tail half the length of the seed itself. Rinse and drain before using in recipe.

Thought for Food

This highly nourishing milk has a desirable live food taste. It is rather perishable, however, so drink it immediately or within twelve hours of preparation to obtain the best flavor and value.

Directory of Nutmilk Ingredients

Most natural food cooperatives and health food stores stock the ingredients found in the recipes. The following distributors supply those retailers. Their mail order catalogs are available for anyone's convenience and you may order certain items direct from the company itself if necessary.

Nuts, Seeds, and Dried Fruit

Jaffe Bros.
28560 Hilac Road
P.O. Box 636
Valley Center, California 92080
(617) 749-1133

Mail order; dried fruits, oils, nuts, seeds, carob powder, etc.

Walnut Acres
Penns Creek, PA 17862
(717) 837-0601

Mail order; high quality; no preservatives, rain forest nuts, organic sunflower seeds and preserves.

Erewhon Inc.
236 Washington Street
Brookline, Massachusetts 02146
(800) 222-8028

Mail order; nuts and nut butters, seeds, etc.

K. B. Hall Ranch
11999 Ojai S.P. Road
Ojai, California 93025
(805) 646-4512

Mail order; preservative free dried apricots and walnuts.

International Protein Industries, Inc.
P.O. Box 871
Smithtown, New York 11787

Chemical free hulled sesame seeds.

Ahlers Organic Data and Grapefruit
Garden
P.O. Box 726
Mecca, California 92254
(619) 396-2337

Mail order; organically grown
dates.

Horizon Natural Products
Soquel, California 95073

Stevia Sweet Leaf Powder

Now Foods
Villa Park, Illinois 60181

Stevia Sweet Leaf Powder.

Es Condido
Box 28
California 92025

Dr. Bronner's Barley Malt &
Calcium Malt Powder.

Juices and Fruit Preserves

Sorrell Ridge Farm
100 Markley Street
Port Reading, New Jersey 07064
(201) 636-2060

Fruit conserves.

Heinke
5365 Clark Road
Paradise, California 95969-6399
(916) 877-4847

Feature: fresh fruit juices with no
sweeteners added.

Special Extras

Red Saffron Herbs
3009 16th Avenue South
Minneapolis, Minnesota 55407

Feature: bee pollen and spices and
slippery elm powder.

American Health Products
El Molino Foods
Ramsey, New Jersey 07446

Carob powder.

Arrowhead Mills
P.O. Box 866
Hereford, Texas 79045
(806) 364-0730

Organically raised flaxseed, whole
unground.

Omega Life Inc.

Flaxseed; ground to powder and
combined with nutritional
cofactors.

Fruitful Yield
4950 W. Oakton
Skokie, Illinois
(312) 679-8975

Feature; guargum (a substitute for
flaxseed if desired).

Flavoring Extracts

Cook Flavoring Co.
Cook's Choice Extracts
P.O. Box 890
Tacoma, Washington 98401
(206) 627-5499

Mail order; retail flavoring extracts in a high quality array of flavors.

Frontier Cooperative Herbs
Box 69
Norway, Iowa 52318

25 natural flavors, all natural, no alcohol or preservatives.

Natural Sweeteners

Lundberg Farms
Richvale, California
95974-0369

Organic Brown Rice Syrup.

Spring Tree Corporation
P.O. Box 1160
Brattleboro, Vermont 05301
(802) 254-8784

Mail order; organic maple syrup & carob powder.